MY TRUE IDENTITY

Harriet Sleigh

RoperPenberthy Publishing Ltd
Horsham, England

Published by RoperPenberthy Publishing Ltd
PO Box 545, Horsham, England

First published in 2004

All scripture quotations, except where otherwise labelled, are from the
New King James Version copyright © 1984 by Thomas Nelson, Inc.

ISBN 1 903905 17 6

Cover design by Angie Moyler

Typeset by Avocet Typeset, Chilton, Aylesbury, Bucks
Printed in the United Kingdom by Bell & Bain Ltd, Scotland

FOREWORD

The life that Jesus Christ came to give us is not bland, boring or dry. It is full of vibrancy, excitement and joy. In other words, Jesus came so we might have genuine fullness of life. That life is like a seed within every born-again Christian. For a person to grow spiritually that life must be appropriated and lived out. A person is transformed by the growth of that life within them. It is not mere intellectual knowledge that transforms a person, it is the revelation of biblical truth by the Holy Spirit in a person's inner being that brings that new life out into the open. The crucifixion, death and resurrection of Jesus Christ have opened up for us a river of new life that is available to all. But we need to learn how to take hold and live in the good of what Jesus has made available to us. In my own life and ministry I have seen the transforming power of God operate through His Word and I know what riches lie in the pages of the bible. In these booklets, Harriet Sleigh provides invaluable tools for the Christian to grow in his or her spiritual life. The principles of scriptural meditation and confession are fundamental to appropriating the life contained in the bible. I encourage you to make full use of these materials and take hold of the abundant life that Jesus died to give you.

Colin Urquhart
October 2004

EATING THE WORD

That which you hold in your hand can transform you to live and walk as Jesus did. God has a glorious purpose for each of His precious children, free from every bondage, walking in the miraculous, in whatever specific area He has called you. How can this be realized? Our growth is dependent on two factors.

Firstly, it depends on the extent to which we want to grow, for Him to increase and us to decrease. If you are content with how you are, do not read on. But if you have a longing from deep within, to live the abundant life He has for you, this is for you.

Secondly, it depends on how much of the Word we yield to so that it takes dominion in our lives, and we live it. Knowing the scriptures just in our minds will have some affect. But it is only if we delight in it, embrace it, letting it affect our whole being, soul and body, and **then live it,** that we truly enter into the abundant life God longs for each of us to walk in.

Scripture clearly tells us that there is a direct relationship between how much we meditate on the Word, and our success (Josh. 1: 8). It is our choice, our responsibility. Through spending time with the Word, in the Word, we come to know it is true on the inside of us. Israel was God's chosen nation, but a generation of them failed to reach the Promised Land because of unbelief (Heb 3; 19). It is knowing the truth in our hearts **within** that sets us free. This life is not a struggle. Praise God it has already been won for us on the cross. As born-again believers, we are now in the Promised Land. We are one with Him as a branch is to a vine. We do not have to fight to possess the promises, but to **discover** what is ours and live it.

As long as we identify with the person we used to be, our old nature, – 'I' have always been like this, although I want to change', our Christian life will be a struggle. This old 'I' is defined by those around us and ourselves. It is essentially separate from God. I may try my hardest to change and become more like Jesus, but make slow progress. This is the traditional way of thinking. It is in fact 'Old Covenant' way of thinking. It involves operating through the tree of the knowledge of good and evil, where the enemy has full access. We evaluate what we have done with criteria independent of God. The enemy, with joy points out where we have failed. He reinforces our deficiency – 'You will never make it', or 'It will not work for you'. It is so easy to feel condemned; then to say the Word does not work, and to justify our failure.

Glory to God, Jesus has set us free, not because of what we have done but because of His shed blood on the cross. The veil separating man from the Father has been destroyed. When Jesus died it was torn in two from top to bottom (Matt 27: 51), the old 'I' was crucified with Him and He has given us a new 'I'. I have a new identity, as His child, born of the Word of God. My unique personality, has received His righteousness, His nature. I have it **now**, with all of His life, His love, joy peace, power etc; now I can live in His presence. I am no longer separate from Him, but abide in Him as a branch does of a vine. It would be madness for a branch to frequently separate itself and then try to rejoin the vine. Similarly for us to see ourselves as separate and then seek God to come into His presence. We are there **now**, all the time. There is no reason to leave. Is this possible? How could this work for me? The essence of this new life is seeing ourselves as having a new 'I' who is no longer separate, but in constant living relationship with the Father, Jesus the Word, and the Holy Spirit.

We are told how this can become a reality for each of us. 'Be transformed by the renewing of our minds', (Rom 12: 2). The word transformed in Greek is 'metamorphoo', the word used to describe the extraordinary transformation of a caterpillar into a butterfly. This analogy may help us to understand and live in this glorious truth of what He has done for us on the cross. We used to be limited and earth-bound, as is a caterpillar. But He has made us into new creations, or a new species, as different from what we used to be as a butterfly is from a caterpillar. 'If anyone is in Christ, he is a new creation; old things have passed away; behold all things have become new', (2 Cor. 5: 17). The tenses show us that this is not a promise but a description of what He has made us, of what we are now.

We are changed as we believe this, let go the old 'caterpillar' mindset, and replace it with that of a 'butterfly' or new creation. The illustration is evocative. A caterpillar crawls with its many legs, is vulnerable to predators, totally earth-bound, and lives its life chewing, struggling. Similarly we used to be self-centred, limited to our natural senses – what we could see or hear etc: Fear was an unwanted companion, fear of not being able to manage, fear of the problems, fear of the future, fear of what others think of us. We are no longer 'caterpillars', but 'butterflies'. The very life of God is in us. Butterflies spend much of their time resting unperturbed. They are not limited by natural laws like the law of gravity, but fly displaying their beauty with which God has clothed them. Glory to God. Similarly when we discover our inheritance, we can rest in it. Struggling is over. We learn how to fly, how to operate in God's supernatural ways, His protection, His supply, divine health, freedom from fear etc: The enemy is beneath our feet, he is defeated, he cannot touch us unless we open the door to him. His only access to us is through our minds. As we learn to fill our minds with the word of God and refuse to give him, with his negative thoughts, any place, he cannot touch us. I begin to speak of myself as my true 'butterfly' identity' 'I am a new creation; I am delivered from the power of darkness'. The Bible, particularly in the epistles, describes our life, the glorious life of the new creation. What He asks us to do He enables. Through the **living Word living in us**, each one of us can 'be', and 'do' all that the Word describes.

The Word has within it inherent power, the awesome power of God to create or accomplish whatever He desires. The Word spoken by God created the world. He sent His Word and healed people. His prophets spoke and kings trembled. Jesus was and is the Word of God. He, who we love, in the form of the Word, is living and powerful, sharper than any two-edged sword. In Acts we are told the Word grew mightily and prevailed. The Holy Scriptures are 'able to make you wise', (2 Tim 3: 15). God is seeking people who tremble at His Word; see its awesome power and yet are drawn to it as a lover is to His beloved. The Holy Spirit, who lives in every born-again believer, is our teacher. He longs to receive the Word, embrace it, so that it vibrates in our hearts, revealing to each of us new glorious revelations, which can ignite within and so transform us, particularly as we step out in faith and live it.

He wants us to **have a beautiful relationship** with Him in many ways, as Lord, Father, husband, friend, and also as the Word, because He is the Word. We are told to love Him with all our heart, with all our soul and with all our strength (Deut 6: 5; and Math 22: 37). If we love Him we love the living Word. We can have a love relationship with the Word. As Jeremiah said, 'Your words were found and I ate them. And your word was to me the joy and rejoicing of my heart' (Jer.15: 16). We are told to draw water from the well of salvation within with joy. With joy we embrace the Word, because we love Him.

We know that the transformation will be glorious; that He will enable each of us to walk in His anointing, His presence, and in His presence is fullness of joy. This can be a reality for us. See yourself living like this. Let this be your personal vision. 'Without vision my people perish', but with it they have a glorious zeal for life. The scripture says that Jesus stood out, in that He had more joy than all his companions. 'As He is so are we in the world', (1 John 4: 17) – this calling is for each of us. When this describes you and me, ordinary believers, our lives will be radiant, they will 'be' revival. Every nation will be impacted.

How much do we believe? The amount that we live! Only as we live the new creation life, which He has purchased for us will He be glorified. We are called to leave the old 'caterpillar' life and **delight in being** a 'butterfly'. We will find it works. It will give us a new zeal for life. Enthusiasm means 'in God'. Being a 'butterfly' will change our expectations; we know that God will be continually intervening on our behalf in glorious ways. It will affect the way we talk and the way we behave. Below is described a way that will mightily assist in enabling you and me to walk just as Jesus did – to get to know and live in our **'true identity'** – Hallelujah!

This is followed by a section called, **'How to live a scripture'**, which will help you to digest and live a particular scripture which has impacted you.

HOW?

By declaring and meditating on who I am and what I can do as a new creation, as described in the scriptures. This is **MY TRUE IDENTITY**, the 'butterfly' life, God ordained for me – hallelujah!

It includes confessions about,

> How I am loved passionately by Almighty God,
> The awesome power of the cross, how I am set free from the past,
> Our new self or new identity – glory to God, I am a blessing,
> The authority that is now mine,
> The day to day walk He expects of every believer,
>   aglow and burning in the Spirit,
> His purpose now embedded in my heart – to glorify our Lord.

By speaking them out regularly and meditating on them, they will become a reality, the way you see yourself, think, and respond whatever the circumstances. Also some of the scriptures are included from which they emerged. Spending time in them will reveal marvelous other dimensions of the truth and so increase your understanding. You will be challenged to delight in finding others to reveal more and more.

As a man thinks in his heart so is he. Your mindset will change to automatically think the truth about yourself as described in the Word. The old negative fearful 'caterpillar' mindset will be replaced by a vibrant, positive glorious one, of who you really are, and God's unique purposes for you. The Holy Spirit will change you, from glory to glory.

There are so many ways that the following declarations can be used to digest these precious truths. They are in large bold to make them easier to read. You could speak some or all of them out, every day. If you do it before you go to sleep your spirit will continue to take hold of them while you sleep. I have found when doing this I sometimes wake up with a glorious revelation –wow! Sometimes I go through them asking God to whisper to me something new about each one, before I go on to the next. I may only 'eat' a few. Next time I can continue. I may speak them out until I come to one that touches my heart and start praying it for myself or for others. The scriptures are there to help the 'feast'. It does not matter which way or ways you choose; it is regularly speaking and meditating on them that will enable the Holy Spirit to take hold of the truth and impact the way you see yourself. Even after one week you will be conscious of a difference. After a month the change will be distinctive. After six months it will be the natural way you think. After that God will continue to reveal more and more of His secrets and mysteries; there is no limit.

The Holy Spirit delights in revealing special insights to each one of us. I share some He has given me in order to encourage you, brother sister, to let Him whisper and reveal glorious facets of the scripture you are feasting on. He longs to do this for you ..... and to walk in it Glory to God!

MY TRUE IDENTITY

Most assuredly, I say to you, unless one is born again, he cannot see the kingdom of God (John 3: 3).

This applies to everyone, whether living on the streets or in a mansion, illiterate or the most learned. No matter how educated we may be, we need to be born again. God made us in His image. He made us to know Him and through this to live a blessed abundant life. Deep within each one of us is the real heart, our spirit, that longs to know God. Through our education we build up many barriers, ideas about ourselves of who we want to be or think we are. We may be very successful in worldly terms, yet inside we know there is more to life. Religion has focused on aspects of ourselves like our past, our qualities, our problems, which infact draw attention to our old 'caterpillar' selves and away from God. He wants to go straight to our heart and meet us there. Glory to God, when we respond, we find that the other problems, the self issues, melt away as we come to know that Almighty God loves us, and longs to do glorious things in and through our lives.

Many know about God, but do you know God, know of His love for you? If not, or you are not sure, right now decide that 'This is for me'. It is only when you are born again that your eyes are open and you are able to see and step into the glorious truths. Be sure you have responded from your heart to His invitation and receive His life.

'For God so loved the world that He gave His only begotten Son, that whoever believes in Him should not perish but have everlasting life.' John 3: 16

'Forgive me Lord, I want to live my life for You alone'. I am saved, born again.

LOVED

Christianity is a beautiful love relationship between us and our Lord. We step from knowing that God loves us because the bible says so, to experiencing it as a glorious ongoing reality. This love relationship is as in marriage. Intimate knowledge of our Lord is acquired. We get to know His heart, His will for us and the joy of living our lives as He directs. It motivates us, instills in us a hunger to know and serve Him more and more. As we get to know Him, He becomes increasingly our security. Our confidence in Him grows, so that we know He will not let us down as we do whatever He asks of us. The first commandment is to love Him with all our heart, soul, strength and mind, so that this can be a reality in our lives.

I had not been a Christian for long, when I found the verse, 1 Peter 1: 8, which reads, 'whom having not seen you love. Though now you do not see Him, yet believing, you rejoice with joy inexpressible and full of glory'. At that time things were not going too well for me and I thought, I would like to have that 'joy unspeakable'. What are the conditions? To love and believe in Him. I do believe, so the issue was truly loving Him. If I was in love with someone, I would be thinking of that person all the time, delighting in them, going over precious moments. I decided to do that with my Lord. I remember walking to a neighbouring farm, saying, with enthusiasm, 'I love You'. I had a distinct warm feeling inside, which I now realize was the Spirit within me delighting in my heart. I walked across the field with a spring in my step – hallelujah! He was encouraging me. The more I thought of Him, and my heart whispered endearments to Him, the more joy welled up from within. When having to do something boring, like a household chore, I would tell Him of my love and that I was doing it for Him, and it no longer was a chore! Now, whatever the circumstance, I know a joy inside. I can love Him always, be in His presence, and the scripture says, in His presence is fullness of joy.

Declarations
1 John 4: 18 There is no fear in love; but perfect love casts out fear, because fear involves torment. But he who fears has not been made perfect in love.

I am loved perfectly
(I know every detail; your strengths, weaknesses, the past, the future. Trust Me; I want to bless you).

Rom 8: 15   For you did not receive the spirit of bondage again to fear, but you received the Spirit of adoption by whom we cry out, 'Abba Father.'
I am loved intimately – 'abba' Father
(The veil is torn, be so open with Me, trust, delight in My embrace).

Is 54: 5   For your Maker is your husband, the Lord of hosts is His name; and your Redeemer is the Holy One of Israel; He is called the God of the whole earth.
– as by a perfect husband
(As the closest love relationship, as 'one'. Let it be, 'we' doing..............)

S of S 8: 6–7   Set me as a seal upon your heart, for love is as strong as death, jealousy as cruel as the grave; its flames are flames of fire, a most vehement flame. Many waters cannot quench love, nor can the floods drown it. If a man would give for love all the wealth of his house, it would be utterly despised.
I am loved passionately as with the very flame of the Lord
(Nothing reserved or held back).

Rom 8: 39   nor height nor depth, nor any other created thing, shall be able to separate us from the love of God which is in Christ Jesus our Lord.
I cannot be separated from Your love
(Whatever the circumstances – no mountain too high or valley too low, I am there with you).

Eph 1: 4   just as He chose us in Him before the foundation of the world, that we should be holy and without blame before Him in love.
I was chosen before the foundation of the world
(You are unique. I have a special glorious purpose already planned for you).

THE OLD HAS GONE

The power of the cross is so glorious. I am free from my past. It is no longer part of me. I do not need deliverance or healing. I am the delivered, the healed. When I look back on it I do so with thanks in my heart – hallelujah!

I am loved perfectly. His hand was on every part of my life; even the tragedies. I went through many hard times. I was unwanted. I married and had two children that died. My husband left me. I learnt so much from Joseph's life he went through much hardship, totally rejected by his brothers, as a slave and then years in prison, before he became ruler of Egypt. But, he was then able to look back on the past and see it from God's perspective; I believe, with thanks in his heart. 'God sent me before you to preserve life..... it was not you who sent me here but God'; and he has made me a father to Pharaoh, and lord of all his house, and ruler throughout all the land of Egypt' (Gen 45: 5, 8).

I wanted to be free from my past. I had to first forgive all those involved; my mother, the doctors, my ex husband. But it was through seeing them as Joseph had done from God's perspective that enabled a total release. The past had to be redefined, so I could even thank Him for the traumatic events. For example, I know I was unwanted by my parents, but that was irrelevant because I was wanted by my heavenly Father. What comfort I can bring to others who have been unwanted. Because two of my children died I see the preciousness of life etc: Now when I look back on the past there are no negatives, no weight. I am free.

So many Christians live their lives trying to be free from their past, not realizing it has already been done for them on the cross. This is the truth. This is what we are saved from. We are free from being self centred struggling 'caterpillars'. We are infact, more than the delivered, or the healed. That person we used to be is no more. Now we can live our lives as new creations, as glorious 'butterflies'.

Declarations

Rom 6: 3–6 Or do you not know that as many of us as were baptized into Christ Jesus were baptized into his death? Therefore we were buried with Him through baptism into death, that just as Christ was raised from the dead by the glory of the Father, even so we also should walk in newness of life. For if we have been united together in the likeness of His death, certainly we also shall be in the likeness of His resurrection, knowing this, that our old man was crucified with Him, that the body of sin might be done away with...

2 Cor 5: 17 Therefore, if anyone is in Christ, he is a new creation; old things have passed away; behold all things have become new.

Gal 2: 20 I have been crucified with Christ; it is no longer I who live, but Christ lives in me; and the life which I now live in the flesh I live by faith in the Son of God who loved me and gave Himself for me.

I (old self centered 'I') **have been crucified with Christ (The person you used to be is no more, that old self-centered independent person full of fear, pride, was buried with Me. When I rose from the dead, so did you as a new creation, a new person).**

Is 43: 1 But now, thus says the Lord, who created you, O Jacob, and He who formed you, O Israel: 'Fear not, for I have redeemed you; I have called you by your name; you are Mine.

Eph 1: 7 In Him we have redemption through His blood, the forgiveness of sins, according to the riches of His grace.

I (new 'I') **have been redeemed through Your blood (It is a perfect redemption. You are free from all the bondages of the curse – fear, oppression, negatives).**

Col 1: 13 He has delivered us from the power of darkness and conveyed us into the kingdom of the Son of His love,

I have been delivered from the power of darkness (As if you no longer lived in the same country; now you are in a new country, new language, new joys).

2 Tim 1: 7   For God has not given us a spirit of fear, but of power and of love and of a sound mind.

1 John 4: 18 There is no fear in love; but perfect love casts our fear, because fear involves torment. But he who fears has not been made perfect in love.

I do not fear
(You are free from the fear of man and the need to worry. My perfect love and power has replaced it. Your security is now in Me, so in its place, delight in an awesome fear of Me).

Rom 6: 14   For sin shall not have dominion over you, for you are not under law but under grace.

Rom 8: 2   For the law of the Spirit of life in Christ Jesus has made me free from the law of sin and death.

I am not under the law but under grace
(The weight of striving to please Me, of failure and success, is now replaced by a delight in doing it for Me).

Is 53: 4–5   Surely He has borne our sicknesses and carried our pains; yet we esteemed Him stricken, smitten by God, and afflicted. But He was wounded for our transgressions, He was bruised for our iniquities; the chastisement for our peace was upon Him, and by His stripes we are healed.

1 Pet 2: 24 who Himself bore our sins in is own body on the tree, that we, having died to sins, might live for righteousness – by whose stripes you were healed.

I have been healed
(The body that used to be sick is no more. Now you have the same divine nature that I have. As I was when on earth, you too are free from sickness, depression, confusion, the past etc).

Gal 5: 1   Stand fast therefore in the liberty by which Christ has made us free, and do not be entangled again with a yoke of bondage.

I am free from every bondage
(I shed My blood because I love you, to cut you loose

from your culture, sin, yourself etc; so you are free to know Me).

Rom 8: 1   There is therefore now no condemnation to those who are in Christ Jesus, who do not walk according to the flesh, but according to the Spirit.
I am free from condemnation
(Know that that nagging accusation is from the enemy and give it no place).

MY NEW SELF

He has made us new creations, a new species, as butterflies are different from caterpillars – hallelujah! It is a glorious truth that we are no longer ordinary people, but the very life of God is throbbing through our bodies. We are born again of the living Word of God, the incorruptible divine seed. The Holy Spirit now vitalizes our mortal bodies. Many Christians live a life trying to become what God has already made them. We just need to believe it, live it, and let go the old mindset. So many have received the lie from the pit that they are of no or very limited value. They therefore expect little from life. The truth is each of us are unique, and so special to our Lord. He has chosen each of us for a glorious purpose.

What a joy it has been to see hundreds of people in Africa and India, who saw themselves as with no hope, no future, forgotten by the world, be transformed by realizing that God had a mighty purpose for them which they could step into. When they give their lives to Jesus, and are filled with the Holy Spirit, their sad faces are transformed; zeal and joy radiate through their eyes.

I easily identify with such people because I saw myself as being of little value. I remember seeing from the scripture (Gen 12: 2), that not only was I blessed, but a blessing. The last thing I saw myself was as a blessing. I remember deciding to take hold of this truth and spoke it out often. After a few days, something within agreed with my words. The challenge was then to live it, to release it. It was a decision. Instead of shrinking when with others, deciding I was going to bless them, with what I said, with a smile, joy or whatever. To my delight I found it worked. What a joy it is to bless. It is so true that it is better to give than to receive, totally contrary to our self centred society which is all out to get. The more we give, the more He pours into us to give – hallelujah! Confessing the truth did not change me into a butterfly, the truth welled up inside, and the old way of thinking fell away. I was not trying to bless, but being a blessing, releasing what was inside of me. There is such a difference, it is **knowing the truth inside** that makes us free.

Declarations

Gen 12: 2   I will make you a great nation; I will bless you and make your name great; and you shall be a blessing.

Eph 1: 3   Blessed be the God and Father of our Lord Jesus Christ, who has blessed us with every spiritual blessing in the heavenly places in Christ.
I am a blessing
(Your new nature has been so mightily blessed with every spiritual blessing. Let them flow naturally from you).

Eph 2: 8   For by grace you have been saved through faith, and that not of yourselves, it is the gift of God.
I live in grace
(Our life is a love relationship; such joy in your heart because you know that My grace will enable you to do whatever I ask of you).

1 Pet 1: 23   having been born again, not of corruptible seed but incorruptible, through the word of God which lives and abides forever.

Rom 8: 11   But if the Spirit of Him who raised Jesus from the dead dwells in you, He who raised Christ from the dead will also give life to your mortal bodies through His Spirit who dwells in you.
I have been born again through the divine incorruptible seed of the word of God
(Your whole being, including your mortal body throbs with My life).

2 Cor 5: 17   Therefore, if anyone is in Christ, he is a new creation; old
things have passed away; behold, all things have become
new.
I am a new creation
(**You are a new species, no longer ordinary, My child; a
new power source is flowing through you**).

Eph 2: 10   For we are His workmanship, created in Christ Jesus for
good works, which God prepared beforehand that we
should walk in them.
I am Your workmanship
(**My work of art; every day as you respond to Me saying,
'Yes Lord', I transform you to become more and more
beautiful**).

1Cor 1:   But of Him you are in Christ Jesus, who became for us
30–31   wisdom from God – and righteousness and sanctification
and redemption – that, as it is written, 'He who glories,
let him glory in the Lord'.
I am in Christ
(**Hidden in Me, part of Me, My body**).

Col 1: 27   To them God willed to make known what are the riches
of the glory of this mystery among the Gentiles: which is
Christ in you the hope of glory.
and **Christ lives in me**
(**All that I am, the fullness of God, lives, throbs in you**).

John 15: 5   I am the vine, you are the branches. He who abides in
Me, and I in him, bears much fruit; for without Me you
can do nothing.

1 Thes 5; 17   pray without ceasing
**I am one with you as a branch is of a vine; we
commune always**
(**No more do you yearn to get into My presence. You are
there. We are one. There is no reason to leave My presence. Let My life flow through you, and bear much fruit**).

Rom 5: 17   For if by the one man's offence death reigned through the
one, much more those who receive abundance of grace

and of the gift of righteousness will reign in life through the One, Jesus Christ.

I have received the gift of Your righteousness
(My nature, not through anything you do, but because of My shed blood. It is a love gift. Now, you are in My Presence with no sense of condemnation or inferiority, and you have the same authority over the enemy which I exercised. We are as one. My nature is in you, so, for example, no more do you try to love; you can 'be' love).

Prov 28: 1   The wicked flee when no one pursues, but the righteous are bold as a lion.

> **– so I am as bold as a lion**
> **(Relying on Me within, you know no fear; expect only victory).**

2 Pet 1: 3–4 ...His divine power has given to us all things that pertain to life and godliness, through the knowledge of Him who called us by glory and virtue, by which have been given to us exceedingly great and precious promises, that through these you may be partakers of the divine nature, having escaped the corruption that is in the world through lust.

I am a partaker of Your divine nature
(My life, the Word is living in you, is you. Like Me, you do not fear, you do not get sick; it is not your nature).

Rom 8: 15–17   For you did not receive the spirit of bondage again to fear, but you received the Spirit of adoption by whom we cry out, 'Abba, Father'. The Spirit Himself bears witness with our spirit that we are children of God, and if children, then heirs – heirs of God and joint heirs with Christ,.....

I am a son/daughter of the King of Kings
(A joint heir with Me, walk as royalty).

Phil 4: 19   And my God shall supply all your need according to His riches in glory by Christ Jesus.

I know You will supply all my needs
(The whole world is Mine. Even in the natural a father tries to supply the needs of his children. Much more will I provide for you my beloved).

John 17: 22 And the glory which You gave Me I have given them, that they may be one just as We are one;

Ps 97: 5 The mountains melt like wax at the presence of the Lord, at the presence of the Lord of the whole earth.

2 Cor 3: 18 But we all, with unveiled face, beholding as in a mirror the glory of the Lord, are being transformed into the same image from glory to glory, just as by the Spirit of the Lord.

I have received Your glory
(So that we can be as one, as I was with My Father. You carry My awesome Presence. My glory is more powerful than any cultural bondage. Mountains melt like wax in the Presence of the Lord. As you focus on Me, I change you from glory to glory).

2 Cor 1: 21 Now He who establishes us with you in Christ and has anointed us is God,

1 John
2: 27 But the anointing which you have received from Him abides in you, and you do not need that anyone teach you; but as the same anointing teaches you concerning all things, and is true, and is not a lie, and just as it has taught you, you will abide in Him.

I am as anointed as You were when on earth
(Exactly the same source of super-natural power, the Holy Spirit, Who lived in Me is now in you. You can be as sensitive to My prompting as I was to My Father, and release whatever is required, as I did.)

1 Cor 2: 16 'For who has known the mind of the Lord that he may instruct Him?' But we have the mind of Christ.

I have Your mind, the mind of Christ
(Transformed by the living word. That old mindset, self-centered, fearful and negative is becoming vibrant, posi-tive and creative).

1 John
16: 13 However, when He, the Spirit of truth, has come, He will guide you into all truth; for He will not speak on His own authority, but whatever He hears He will speak; and He will tell you things to come.

1 Cor 2: 12   Now we have received, not the spirit of the world, but the Spirit who is from God, that we might know the things that have been freely given to us by God.
I am able to understand the Truth and mysteries
(Delight in the truth, be so expectant and I will reveal My heart to you).

John 10: 27 My sheep hear My voice, and I know them, and they follow Me.
I hear Your voice
(Expect Me to guide, prompt, even speak to you twenty four hours a day, whatever you are doing).

Is 12: 2–3   Behold, God is my salvation, I will trust and not be afraid; 'For Yah, the Lord, is my strength and song; He also has become my salvation.' Therefore with joy you will draw water from the wells of salvation.

John 4: 14   … But the water that I shall give him will become in him a fountain of water springing up into everlasting life.

John 7: 38   He who believes in Me , as the Scripture has said, out of his heart will flow rivers of living water
I draw water with joy from the well of salvation within
(All of Me, My love, joy, peace, wisdom, power, healing, forgiveness etc, is within you. Continually draw from it with joy, with confidence, and release it).

Rom 12: 3   For I say, through the grace given to me, to everyone who is among you, not to think of himself more highly than he ought to think, but to think soberly, as God has dealt to each one a measure of faith.

Rom 1: 17   For in it (the gospel) the righteousness of God is revealed from faith to faith; as it is written, 'The just shall live by faith'.
I have Your faith within
(a divinely implanted measure of faith – use it so that it grows from faith to faith).

1Cor 1: 30   But of Him you are in Christ Jesus, who became for us wisdom from God – and righteousness and sanctification and redemption –
I have Your wisdom within
(Expect it to flow when you draw it up from the well within).

Rom 5: 5   Now hope does not disappoint, because the love of God has been poured out in our hearts by the Holy Spirit who was given to us.
I have Your love within
(Including My zeal. It compels you be that chosen vessel through whom My glorious purposes are realized. I implore you to release it to bless this hungry desolate world).

John 14: 27 Peace I leave with you, My peace I give to you; not as the world gives do I give to you. Let not your heart be troubled, neither let it be afraid.
I have Your peace within
(Such confidence in Me, wholeness, rest).

John 15: 11 These things I have spoken to you, that My joy may remain in you, and that your joy may be full.
Neh 8: 10   .....Do not sorrow, for the joy of the Lord is your strength.
I have Your joy within
(The fruit of being one with Me as two lovers and it is your strength in any circumstance).

Prov 29: 18 Where there is no revelation (prophetic vision), the people cast off restraint; but happy is he who keeps the law.
I have a vision
(Let it be a driving force, to walk just as I walked, with all the supernatural gifts flowing. Seek Me re your individual vision and then ardently pursue it. Keep it burning, do not let the enemy quench it).

AUTHORITY

Few Christians realize, know inside the truth that the enemy has been totally defeated. He has no power over us other than what we give him. He is excellent at deceiving, but if we refuse to receive his lies and keep the door closed, he is no problem. We know his strategies. He tries to get our focus off God and onto ourselves, (as he did in the garden of Eden). Then he encourages us to rebel against God, to do things our way, independently of Him. Another ploy is to get us to fear, indeed to have more faith in the negative reports which he instigates rather than in the truth, the Word of God. It is so important for our mindset to change from being a victim of circumstances to being able to change those circumstances, to rise up, take responsibility and dominion and to rule (Rom 5: 17).

We need to speak aggressively to the enemy when he attacks, so that he knows we will tolerate no nonsense. When in India and Zambia I taught the Christians, some of whom had just given their lives to God, to use this authority. I taught them to use it to make sure the enemy could have no place in their lives. They would loudly, aggressively declare, 'In Jesus Name – go!', with the same ruthlessness they would use if a dog or a goat had come into their house. When they did this the enemy ran from them terrified. They applied this to the spirit of poverty which is so much part of their culture. Then they would speak in the truth, that 'I am rich'. I taught them how to stand on the blessings of Abraham, which declare that whatever they put their hand to will prosper etc: They knew they were free. They also used their authority to rebuke any sickness; to command it to leave them and to speak in the truth that they are healed. Many, at one meeting about 40% of them, wanted to testify to distinct changes in their bodies. What was so exciting for me was the testimonies that followed. For example, one person shared the following week how her child had been very ill, and how she had laid hands on her and told the sickness to go. Immediately the child asked for food! God wants every born-again believer to walk in the authority He has purchased for us. By so doing we reveal Jesus and the glorious life of freedom He has purchased for us. Our lives and speech must not just be in words, but in the demonstration of His power. Our lives will attract others to our Lord. God intends this to be the natural life of a 'butterfly' or a new creation.

Declarations

Col 2: 15   Having disarmed principalities and powers, He made a public spectacle of them, triumphing over them in it.
I know You have defeated the enemy; You triumphed over him
(Now you are in Me, so make the decision never to be defeated by him).

Math 28: 18 And Jesus came and spoke to them, saying, 'All authority has been given to Me in heaven and on earth'.

Eph 1: 20–21 ...He raised Him(Jesus)from the dead and seated Him at His right hand in the heavenly places, far above all principality and power and might and dominion, and every name that is named, not only in this age but also in that which is to come.

Eph 2: 6   ....and raised us up together, and made us sit together in the heavenly places in Christ Jesus.
I am seated together with You in heavenly places at the Father's right hand, the place of authority
(You died with me, were buried with Me and rose together with Me with the same resurrection life. It is a spiritual law that a lower authority always has to bow to a higher one.When on earth I demonstrated this authority over the enemy and nature. You have this same authority.

Luke 10: 19 Behold I give **you** the authority to trample on serpents and scorpions, and over all the power of the enemy, and nothing shall by any means hurt you.
I have been given this authority to trample on serpents and scorpions and over all the power of the enemy.
(re all aspects of the curse – sickness, depression, fear etc: Walk in this authority purchased for you. the enemy is under your feet. Whatever form he tries to take, decide he will become as dust. Do not just be defensive. What are you going to tread on today?)

James 4: 7   Therefore submit to God. Resist the devil and he will flee from you.
I resist the devil and he has to flee
(He is as terrified of you as he was of Me when you stand in and use that authority).

Phil 2: 9–10   Therefore God also has highly exalted Him and given Him the name which is above every name, that at the name of Jesus every knee should bow, of those in heaven, and of those on earth, and of those under the earth,
I use the Name of Jesus knowing every knee must bow to the King of Kings
(– it is as if I am speaking).

Mark 11: 23   For assuredly, I say to you, whoever says to this mountain, 'Be removed and be cast into the sea,' and does not doubt in his heart, but believes that those things he says will be done, he will have whatever he says.

Math 17: 20   ....if you have faith as a mustard seed, you will say to this mountain, 'Move from here to there,' and it will move; and nothing will be impossible for you.
I speak to mountains (problems) and they are removed
(Know the authority in your mouth; nothing is impossible for you).

2 Cor 10:
4–5   For the weapons of our warfare are not carnal but mighty in God for pulling down strongholds, casting down arguments and every high thing that exalts itself against the knowledge of God, bringing every thought into captivity to the obedience of Christ,
I demolish strongholds, old mindsets
('You' trying, good works, pride, etc. Imagine dynamite placed under the wall and see it explode).

1 John 5: 4   For whatever is born of God overcomes the world. And this is the victory that has overcome the world – our faith.

2 Cor 2: 14   Now thanks be to God who always leads us in triumph in Christ, and through us diffuses the fragrance of His knowledge in every place.

Heb 3: 6　　…And it is we who are [now members] of this house, if we hold fast and firm to the end our joyful and exultant confidence and sense of triumph in our hope [in Christ]. (Amplified Bible)
I am an overcomer; victory is certain – with joy I hold fast to Your Word
(Fight the fight of faith, refuse to accept defeat).

Rom 8: 37　Yet in all these things we are more than conquerors through Him who loved us.
I am more than a conqueror
(Not just a conqueror; the issue is what to do with the spoils).

Josh 1: 3　Every place that the sole of your foot will tread upon I have given you….
Every place that the sole of my foot will tread upon will be possessed for You
(Expect that wherever I take you, darkness will be destroyed, and My light, My glory released).

Num 14: 9　Only do not rebel against the Lord, nor fear the people of the land, for they are our bread; their protection has departed from them, and the Lord is with us. Do not fear them.

2 Cor 3: 18　But we all with unveiled face, beholding as in a mirror the glory of the Lord, are being transformed into the same image from glory to glory, just as by the Spirit of the Lord.
The enemy is as bread to me
(What are you going to eat today My beloved? And thereby grow strong through victory after victory).

Rom 5: 17　For if by one man's offence death reigned through the one, much more those who receive abundance of grace and of the gift of righteousness will reign in life through the One, Jesus Christ.

Math 10: 8　Heal the sick, cleanse the lepers, raise the dead, cast out demons. Freely you have received, freely give.

I reign as a king in life
(Rule, speak to your body, relationships and circumstances, destroy the works of the enemy, release the kingdom of God).

Mark 11: 22   So Jesus answered and said to them, 'Have faith in God,' (in Greek, 'Have the God kind of faith')

Rom 4: 17   ....God who gives life to the dead and calls those things which do not exist as though they did:
I call things which do not exist as though they did.
(This is the creative power of your words).

Eph 6: 11   Put on the whole armour of God, that you may be able to stand against the wiles of the devil.
I wear and use the armour of God
(Stand in the fullness of what I have given you and refuse to be moved).

Deut 28: 13   And the Lord will make you the head and not the tail; you shall be above only, and not be beneath, if you heed the commandments of the Lord your God....

1 John 4: 4   You are of God, little children, and have overcome them, because He who is in you is greater than he who is in the world.
I am the head and not the tail
(The strongest spirit dominates, and greater is He that is in you, than he that is in the world. Do not tolerate any work of the enemy).

Eph 4:
26–27   'Be angry, and do not sin': do not let the sun go down on your wrath, nor give place to the devil.

Rom 12: 9   Let love be without hypocrisy. Abhor what is evil. Cling to what is good.
I am angry at what the enemy has done, hate what is evil, and refuse to be lulled to sleep and compromise
(Let My love in you stir up righteous anger instilling a passion to release those in bondage).

James 1: 2–4   My brethren, count it all joy when you fall into various trials, knowing that the testing of your faith produces patience. But let patience have its perfect work, that you may be perfect and complete, lacking nothing.

Acts 4: 29–30
'Now, Lord, look on their threats, and grant to Your servants that with all boldness they may speak Your word, by stretching out Your hand to heal and that signs and wonders may be done through the name of Your holy Servant Jesus'.

I see trials as new challenges, and rejoice in them (You know I will intervene gloriously).

WALK

Our walk is an expression of who we are. Our lives should be an epistle, or an illustration of the Word of God; the Word now living in our flesh. No more do we try to love or be victorious, as we did when we were 'caterpillars'. It is the nature of a 'butterfly' to love and to be victorious. We are love, are overcomers. The scriptures say it, we believe, receive it and live it. If insufficient love seems to be flowing, we do not ask for more as all His love is within. No, we ask for more to be released. If we have suffered defeat, we now realise that victory is our inheritance, and refuse to accept defeat any more. God's people are destroyed not through the enemy but through lack of knowledge. Now we know, so we can simply ask forgiveness for accepting the lies of the enemy in any area, and decide in our hearts never again to listen to those lies but to accept only victory. Then we start applying the Word; start speaking out the desired outcome, receiving it, thanking God for it, becoming pregnant with it. This is putting the Word to work.

I have found that **this can be applied to our emotions too.** When we lived as 'caterpillars', so much of our energy was wasted. It leaked away in worry, fear, etc. As our minds are renewed we discover we are commanded not to worry (Math 6: 25); butterflies are free from it. In the same way we have brought our mind into the captivity of Christ, to think only as the Word describes, we can do the same with our emotions, so that our emotional energy is not leaked away. Our heart, our desires, motives, are of key importance to God. 'Keep your heart with all diligence, for out of it spring the issues of life' (Prov 4: 23).

We are commanded to love Him with all of our heart and love

28

others with the same love. Our whole life can be an expression of such a heart, all we do and think. I have found that by surrendering any other emotions, fear, worry, lust, we can walk free of them, standing in victory in those areas. A beautiful fruit of doing this is having so much more energy. It is not wasted. It is being used as the God who made us intended it to be used, loving Him with all our hearts and others with the same love. Some people feel they do not want to give up their 'pleasure on-the-side', their addiction is sweet – so the enemy has persuaded them. Once they see the glorious freedom, the fullness of joy which is their portion, as they live their lives as God intended, the deception of the enemy has no more weight. 'Butterflies' live an abundant life in every area, not hidden, visible for all to see, Hallelujah! I believe when those in the world see the fire of His love, His life burning in us, they will not be able to resist Him. 'The whole earth is eagerly waiting for the revealing of the sons of God' (Rom 8: 19).

Declarations

Deut 6: 5   You shall love the Lord your God with all your heart, with all your soul, and with all your strength.

Math 22: 37 Jesus said to him, 'You shall love the Lord your God with all your heart, with all your soul, and with all your mind'.
I love You with all my heart, all my soul and all my strength
(**nothing left over**).

1 Pet 1: 8, 9 whom having not seen you love. Though now you do not see Him, yet believing, you rejoice with joy inexpressible and full of glory, receiving the end of your faith – the salvation of your souls.
I love You so I am filled with an inexpressible, triumphant and heavenly joy
(**Involves your mind, will, emotions, body so this is total salvation, nothing left out – I love it**).

Rom 5: 5   Now hope does not disappoint, because the love of God has been poured out in our hearts by the Holy Spirit who was given to us.

Eph 3: 19   to know the love of Christ which passes knowledge; that
            you may be filled with all the fullness of God.
            **I am getting to know Your love for me and experi-
            encing being filled with all Your fullness**
            (If not living in My fullness, there is more to know....).

Ps 40: 8   'I delight to do Your will, O my God, and Your law is
            within my heart'.
            I delight to do Your will,
1 Thess 5: 16   Rejoice always.
                        – rejoicing always

Jer 31: 33 But this is the covenant that I will make with the house of
            Israel after those days, says the Lord: I will put My law in
            their minds, and write it on their hearts; and I will be
            their God, and they shall be My people.
Rom 8: 2   For the law of the Spirit of life in Christ Jesus has made
            me free from the law of sin and death.
Phil 2:   .....work out your own salvation with fear and trembling;
12–13   for it is God who works in you both to will and to do for
            His good pleasure.
            I delight in Your laws that are in my heart.
            **(They are part of you and work in you, motivate you to
            love and to walk as I did when on earth) – hallelujah!**

Matt 22: 39   And the second (great commandment) is like it; 'You shall
              love your neighbour as yourself'.
              I love others with the same (passionate) **love,**
Math 6: 15   But if you do not forgive men their trespasses, neither will
              your Father forgive your trespasses.
                        – and am quick to forgive
                        (To restore love).

1 John 4: 4   You are of God, little children, and have overcome them,
              because He who is in you is greater than he who is in the
              world.
              I walk in the power of Your love

(My love in you is greater, above the self-centredness in the world).

Rom 12: 11 Never lag in zeal and in earnest endeavour; be aglow and burning with the Spirit, serving the Lord (Amplified Bible).
I am aglow, burning in the spirit serving You
(With joy and zeal).

Prov 4: 23 Keep your heart with all diligence, for out of it spring the issues of life.
I keep my heart with all diligence
(Not to grieve Me; no trace of pride or self-thoughts).

Gal 5: 16 I say then: Walk in the Spirit, and you shall not fulfil the lust of the flesh.
I walk in the Spirit,

Rom 8: 14 For as many as are led by the Spirit of God, these are sons of God.
– am led by the Spirit

Eph 5: 18 And do not be drunk with wine, in which is dissipation; but be filled with the Spirit,
– and filled with the Spirit
(In harmony with Me, 100% submitted; always expectant of Me).

2 Cor 4: 18 while we do not look at the things which are seen, but at the things which are not seen. For the things which are seen are temporary, but the things which are not seen are eternal.

Rom 8: 5–6 For those who live according to the flesh set their minds on the things of the flesh, but those who live according to the Spirit, the things of the Spirit. For to be carnally minded is death, but to be spiritually minded is life and peace.
I focus on things unseen; my mind is set on things of the Spirit (My glorious purposes. The effect is life and peace).

1 Sam 16: 7 But the Lord said to Samuel, 'Do not look at his appearance or at his physical stature, because I have refused him. For the Lord does not see as man sees; for man looks at the outward appearance, but the Lord looks at the heart.

2 Cor 5: 16 Therefore, from now on, we regard no one according to the flesh. Even though we have known Christ according to the flesh, yet now we know Him thus no longer.
I do not respond to the appearance of others, but their hearts
(their relationship with Me and how to encourage them).

John 4: 24 God is Spirit, and those who worship Him must worship in spirit and truth'.
I worship in spirit and truth
(Draw with joy from the spirit within. It is the love language of your heart: it can be expressed in so many ways. With all your heart soul and body embrace Me and the Word, so there is harmony in you, no hypocrisy. It will be as an open heaven; like an electric circuit open to the source of your life).

1 Thes 5: 17 pray without ceasing
– praying always
(Switched on continually, whatever you are doing).

Phil 4: 13 I can do all things through Christ who strengthens me.
I know that I can do all things You ask of me through the anointing within
(No limit – All of My glorious power will flow as required).

Prov 3: 5 Trust in the Lord with all your heart, and lean not on your own understanding;
I trust You with all my heart
(You rely on Me, you know I am faithful).

John 1: 1, 14 In the beginning was the Word, and the Word was with God, and the Word was God. And the Word became flesh and dwelt among us, and we beheld His glory, the glory as of the only begotten of the Father, full of grace and truth.

I trust the Word, the Truth, as You are the Word (rest your weight on it).

Is: 66: 2　But on this one will I look; on him who is poor and of a contrite spirit, and who trembles at My word'.

I tremble at Your word
(your heart saying, 'Yes Lord'. It reveals My awesome glorious power – receive it by faith and do it).

Jer 15: 16　Your words were found, and I ate them, and Your word was to me the joy and rejoicing of my heart;

I feast on the Word; it is the joy and rejoicing of my heart
(Embrace it, eat it, and digest it, so that it ignites within).

Heb 4: 12　For the word of God is living and powerful, and sharper than any two-edged sword, piercing even to the division of soul and spirit, and of joints and marrow, and is a discerner of the thoughts and intents of the heart.

> **– it is living and powerful, sharper than any two-edged sword**
> **(It penetrates the depths of your heart, able to change you, release you – Glory to God!).**

1 Thes 2: 13　....the word of God which you heard from us, you welcomed it not as the word of men, but as it is in truth, the word of God, which also effectively works in you who believe.

> **– it is working effectively in me**
> **(Expect miracles daily).**

Acts 19: 20　So the word of the Lord grew mightily and prevailed.

> **– it is prevailing**
> **(lives and situations are changing).**

Rom 4: 20–21　He did not waver at the promise of God through unbelief, but was strengthened in faith, giving glory to God, and being fully convinced that what He had promised He was also able to perform.

I do not stagger at Your promise but embrace it with joy
(Know that I long for you to receive it. This is the fight of faith, through which you will grow strong).

Mark 11: 24 Therefore I say to you, whatever things you ask when you pray, believe that you receive them, and you will have them.
I pray, speak out the Word and receive it now
(Even if not evident, possess it, be pregnant with it; declare it done, give thanks for it).

Prov 18: 21 Death and life are in the power of the tongue, and those who love it will eat its fruit.
I know life and death are in the power of my tongue
(Only speak out good positive words, and they will come into being. Never speak negatively).

1 Thes 5: 18 in everything give thanks; for this is the will of God in Christ Jesus for you.
I give thanks in everything
(For My presence with you, and in trials for the outcome which you speak into being).

2 Cor 5: 7 For we walk by faith, not by sight,
Heb 11: 6 But without faith it is impossible to please Him, for he who comes to God must believe that He is, and that He is a rewarder of those who diligently seek Him.
1 Pet 1: 7 .... the genuineness of your faith, being much more precious than gold that perishes, though it is tested by fire, may be found to praise, honour, and glory at the revelation of Jesus Christ,
I walk by faith, not by sight
(Stand on the promise, not affected by circumstances or feelings).

Heb 4: 3, 10 For we who have believed do enter that rest,....
For he who has entered His rest has himself also ceased from his works as God did from His.

I believe, so I have entered Your rest and ceased from struggling
(Now, your confidence is in Me; you rely on Me, on the Word. Your life is becoming a manifestation of the Word).

Gal 6: 14   But God forbid that I should boast except in the cross of our Lord Jesus Christ, by whom the world has been crucified to me, and I to the world.
I glory, even boast in the power of the cross and the power of Your blood
(Look at what I and your Father have done for you – the glorious abundant life now yours).

John 15: 5   I am the vine, you are the branches. He who abides in Me, and I in him, bears much fruit; for without Me you can do nothing.
I abide in You, Your word, so I produce much fruit
(fruit that remains).

1 John 2: 6   He who says he abides in Him ought himself also to walk just as He walked.
– and walk just as You did,

Mk 16: 17, 18   And these signs will follow those who believe; In My name they will cast out demons; they will speak with new tongues; they will take up serpents; and if they drink anything deadly, it will by no means hurt them; they will lay hands on the sick, and they will recover.
– casting out demons,
(The Spirit in you is greater than he in the world and must bow to My Word).
– laying hands on the sick and seeing them recover
(through touch, releasing My Spirit to evict the spirit that sustains the sickness).

John 7: 38   'He who believes in Me, as the Scripture has said, out of his heart will flow rivers of living water.'

Is 11: 2–3   The Spirit of the Lord shall rest upon Him, the Spirit of wisdom and understanding, the Spirit of counsel and

might, the Spirit of knowledge and of the fear of the Lord. His delight is in the fear of the Lord...
I release continually rivers of living water
(drawing from the well of salvation, the fullness of Your spirit and Your life).

Ezek 47: 9   And it shall be that every living thing that moves, wherever the rivers go, will live. There will be a very great multitude of fish, because these waters go there; for they will be healed, and everything will live wherever the river goes.
– bringing life wherever I go
(My love flowing from you, melting hearts, and just as I did opening eyes, releasing captives).

PURPOSE

What freedom it is that the focus of my life is not what I make of it, but that God, Almighty God will use it to the full with His resources. It is not important what other people think of me, so I am not controlled by them. I am not trying to become someone in my own strength, always evaluating and finding that I fail or come short of what I desire. No, no, I long for others to know, to walk in His glorious light, freedom. Each one of us has their own particular calling or area where there is a distinctive anointing. We know that it can only be realized through the very life of God throbbing, flowing through us and it will bear glorious fruit. So with joy we delight to do what He asks of us, knowing He will intervene............ What a life!

I have found that a beautiful outcome of my heart being united with my Lord's, is to discover that so many brothers and sisters throughout the world have the same heart. Factors which normally divide are irrelevant. What joy it is to find that I am one with an Indian or African, irrespective of the fact that for so many of them, food on the table next day is uncertain or that nine of them live in one room. Glory to God! I praise and thank Him that once they have heard the truth, they are discovering for themselves the blessings of Abraham which are theirs. Their situations are changing. There is a new joy in their hearts. They are stepping into the inheritance God longs for every believer to possess. The river of God is flowing from them and they are becoming blessings to others – Hallelujah!

Declarations

Exod 19: 5–6   Now therefore, if you will indeed obey My voice and keep My covenant, then you shall be a special treasure to Me above all people; for all the earth is Mine, and you shall be to Me a kingdom of priests and a holy nation'...

1 Pet 2: 9   But you are a chosen generation, a royal priesthood, a holy nation, His own special people, that you may proclaim the praises of Him who called you out of darkness into His marvelous light;
For You to be glorified
(In everything you think, speak and do – open heaven).

Math 6: 10   Your kingdom come. Your will be done on earth as it is in heaven.
To establish Your kingdom on earth
(All knowing Me, the Word, and living it).

1 John 3: 8   ...For this purpose the Son of God was manifested, that He might destroy the works of the devil.
To destroy the works of the enemy
(That have tied up so many).

Luke 4: 18   The Spirit of the Lord is upon Me, because He has anointed Me to preach the gospel to the poor; He has sent Me to heal the brokenhearted, to proclaim liberty to the captives and recovery of sight to the blind, to set at liberty those who are oppressed;

Mark 16: 20   And they went out and preached everywhere, the Lord working with them and confirming the word through the accompanying signs. Amen.
To preach the gospel
(expecting miracles to confirm the Word),
To release captives, open blind eyes and heal the broken hearted
(Expect divine encounters).

37

John 17: 18 Just as You sent Me into the world, I also have sent them into the world (Amplified Bible).

To walk as You did when on earth, revealing Your glory

(Walking on water, with no props – manifesting the same God given love and authority; doing the same glorious things).

HOW TO LIVE A SCRIPTURE

The Word of God is BRILLIANT

It is glorious to have the **Living Word** inside us, to know the truth of the Word deep within. Then when we speak the Word, the situation is changed, the person is healed, we find the job, relationships are restored etc:

'Is not My Word like a fire?' says the Lord, 'And like a hammer that breaks in pieces the rock (of most stubborn resistance)?' Jer 23: 29 (Amplified Bible).

What joy it is to step into the Word, to possess it, to live it. In Luke 4: 21 Jesus announced that **'Today this Scripture is fulfilled in your hearing'**. Jesus stepped into that scripture. In other words, He said 'This Scripture describes Me'. We can similarly make any scripture our possession; especially those describing who we are as new creations or ones that have particularly touched our heart.

I have made use of the word **'BRILLIANT'** to help us to digest a specific scripture and live it out. The **Word** is **brilliant** in what it can do in and through us. The consonants in **'BRILLIANT'** can be used to provide a structure for this.

BELIEVE	Know it is the living Word, spoken by Almighty God
RECEIVE	Possess it personally with joy
LIVE IT evident in	Language – speak it out
LIVE IT evident in	Lifestyle – changing the way you behave
NOW	Today release it, use it
TRIUMPHANTLY	Know it works

How does it work?

Take a particular scripture, one that has spoken to you, or perhaps one of the Declarations in "My True Identity". Then use it as follows;

BELIEVE
Know it is the living Word, spoken by Almighty God.
Tremble at His word. Thank Him for the truth.
Believe as a child believes.
Lay aside the old negative thinking of the world.
Let Him speak to you as if He is in the room with you.

RECEIVE
Possess it with **Joy** personally, with a **thankful heart**.
Put your name in the scripture.
Again give no place to your old way of thinking.
Receive it deep inside with such joy.
Delight in it – meditate on it.
Speak it out often, softly, loudly.
Know as you do, as you say the same as the Scriptures, you will become more and more confident and excited about it.
A young child given a strange present, may look at it from different angles, touch it, explore it. All his attention is focused on it, so he gets to know it, even before using it.
You can similarly explore and delight in the truth.
Use your mind to the full; what does this word mean?
Are there any other similar scriptures?
The Holy Spirit Who lives in you will help to reveal the glory of the truth.

LIVE IT evident in my   **Language** –
Decide, I will delight in speaking out this truth, sharing with others its beauty, excitement...

LIVE IT evident in my   **Lifestyle** –

        Decide to put it to work. I will no longer react as
        I always have done.
        I now **know** the truth so there will be **victory** in
        this area.

NOW   **Today** my life will be different. Think of specific
        times or places, or issues, which will not be the
        same – Hallelujah!

TRIUMPHANTLY Know it will happen.
        Be so **expectant** that the Holy Spirit, who is living
        in you, will move mightily in you to see that it
        happens – that it will be a reality today.

Example 1

There is no fear in love; but perfect love casts out fear, because fear
involves torment. He who fears has not been made perfect in love
(1 John 4: 18).

'I am loved perfectly'

Believe

It is so glorious, that I am loved perfectly by Almighty God. As I get to
know this truth **inside**, I will be free of fear, of people, circumstances
etc: – praise God!

The Scriptures show His love. It is there throughout the Old
Testament. His people rebelled again and again, but God longed for
them to return to Him so He could bless them. '**I will heal their back-
sliding, I will love them freely, for my anger has turned away from him
(Israel)**' (Hos14: 4). This perfect love is shown in the Gospels. How He
sent His precious Son to die, so that all of us who have gone our own
way could know Him, and receive the extraordinary inheritance He
has won for us. Almighty God had, and always has had, wonderful
plans for His own children. That means for me. These plans can only
be mine if I believe and respond to this beautiful love. **I will believe it!**

Thank You Lord for this truth. It is the **living Word of Almighty
God**. I tremble at Your Word; I dare not disagree with any part of it. I

will give no place to my old 'caterpillar' mind, full of negatives, and fear. I will believe Your truth as a child believes – and trusts. I will believe it as if You were standing in the room speaking to me – Thank You Lord.

Receive
With **joy** and such a thankful heart I receive this love. I believe what Your Word says, that **God Almighty loves me (my name)**, that **I am so precious to Him**. Thank You Lord. Let joy rise up from within. What peace and confidence it gives me.

I will delight in Your love and think much about what it means for me. I am loved perfectly. I will speak it often, softly – whisper it so it sinks deep into my heart. You are with me always, I can never be alone. Nothing can separate me from Your love. I have been through tough times, but You were with me, You brought me through. You know every detail about my life, my strengths and weaknesses, successes and failures, and yet You still love me. Even more glorious is that You want to bless me. I will speak it loudly, declaring it, or even sing it – You have glorious plans for me – wow!

How can I fear when I know You love me perfectly and You are with me always? I will totally trust in this glorious truth.

Live it – Language
I will not keep to myself how wonderful it is to know that I am loved by You. I may even sing about You – not just when alone! I will encourage others to know this beautiful love for themselves – Hallelujah

Live it – Lifestyle
I will not hide this joy in my heart. I will have a new twinkle in my eye. I will be ready to share about why I have this inner joy and confidence with anyone I meet.

I have been frightened of my (husband, boss, child, work etc:) but not now. When I see them there will be such peace in my heart, such confidence in You.

I will be able to love them with Your love. I know You will give me the words to say – praise God!

Now

Today I will be different, when by myself, on the way to work, while working, in the shops, wherever I am there will be a new joy in my heart. I refuse to fear. …Instead I expect You to protect me, to give me wisdom or whatever I need.

Triumphantly

I know it will work. I am so expectant. I know others will see a difference in me and be drawn to You as a result – praise God!

I will no longer be the victim, but will shine with Your love, Your life. The situation will be changed – glory to God!

Example 2

Behold, I give you the authority to trample on serpents and scorpions, and over all the power of the enemy, and nothing shall by any means hurt you (Luke 10: 19).

I have been given authority to trample of serpents and scorpions and over all the power of the enemy,

Believe

When Jesus was on earth, people were amazed at the authority with which He spoke. All authority had been given to Him, and He used it over the enemy, casting out demons, healing the sick, stilling the storm etc: On the cross Jesus defeated the enemy for us. He triumphed over him – glory to God! He has given this same authority to us. I give you authority – over **all** the power of the enemy. The enemy is the author of all aspects of the curse, fear, sickness, depression poverty etc: We have been given authority to trample on, and to destroy any evidence of them in our lives, and in the lives of those around us. To do this He has given us His Name, so that when we speak it, it is as if Jesus was speaking. Also we are told that if we resist the enemy, as we rebuke him, he has to flee, or run in terror (James 4: 7) – glory to God. As we stand in these glorious truths, nothing can possibly harm us. This is Your Word. This is the truth. I will believe it.

Receive

Thank You Lord, that You have given me (my name) this authority. I will meditate on these glorious truths until I know them deep within. I will speak them out often; 'The same authority that You walked in, I walk in. It is over all the power of the enemy. You have given it to me **to use**, to put to work'. In the Old Testament Your people had to plead for You to take action, for You to remove the problem. Now it is my responsibility. You ask me to speak to the problem with a prayer of faith, not doubting in my heart, and know that it has to move (Mark 11; 23). Thank You Lord that nothing of the curse is greater than Your Name. If sickness arises, I can rebuke it, 'In the Name of Jesus go', and it has to go. Then I declare, 'I am healed'. If fear tries to fill my heart, I can speak out, 'I refuse to fear', and declare the truth, eg: 'Thank You Lord I have not a spirit of fear but of power, and of love and of a sound mind' (2 Tim 1: 7). 'Thank You Lord that You have made me free, so I am free – hallelujah!' I will use this authority in whatever form or place I see the enemy active. I declare 'victory over all the devices of the enemy'. For myself, 'I will tolerate no area of bondage, no sickness, no depression. I will receive no negative thoughts about myself.

I refuse to give place to any unbelief. I refuse to fear, I refuse to be sick – hallelujah! I thank You Lord that I am more than a conqueror – greater is He that is in me than he that is in the world – that You always lead me in triumph – praise Your glorious Name!

Live it – Language

I will seek opportunities to tell others about these truths. My language will have no negatives. I will speak of victory and encourage others to see it. More than that God wants every believer to use this authority He has given us so that they too can **walk in the reality** of the freedom He purchased for us, the abundant life, free of all the oppression and bondage of the enemy – glory to God!

Live it – Lifestyle

There is a particular area in my life where I need victory today (name it).

I declare to you, enemy, that you are going to be ground into the earth as dust. There will be 100% victory in this area. I will be so full of expectation. Others will see my confidence in You, Lord, and that it works, that it impacts everyday life. They will be drawn to You.

What joy it will be to come alongside others going through the same problem and encourage them.

Now
Today, I have received a trickle of unbelief in (name the area). Forgive me Lord. If it arises again, I will aggressively rebuke it in Jesus Name, and speak out the truth – what You have specifically said, or promised in Your Word – with such joyful confidence (Heb 3: 6b). In fact, if such thoughts arise, I will take it as a prompt to elaborate more on the desired result. I know You will reveal more. I am excited already. The enemy will be sorry he tried to implant such thoughts – glory to God!

Triumphantly
I am so full of **expectation**; victory will be my song – hallelujah. There will be many testimonies as the result of today – glory to God!

Example 3
For this reason we also thank God without ceasing, because when you received the word of God which you heard from us, you welcomed it not as the word of men, but as it is in truth, the word of God, which also effectively works in you who believe. 1Thes 2: 13.

The Word of God is working effectively in me

Believe
It is the Spirit who gives life: the flesh profits nothing. The words that I speak to you are spirit and they are life (John 6: 63). The Word of God received by a rational, carnal mind is of no value, but received by the Spirit of God in us, becomes life in us and through us – wow! For the word of God is living and powerful, and sharper than any two-edged sword, piercing even to the division of soul and spirit, and of joints and marrow, and is a discerner of the thoughts and intents of the heart (Heb 4: 12). God wants His Word **to live in us** so that it works effectively. In the Greek the word effective is 'energeo' from which energy derives. It means 'the active operation or **working of power** and its **effectual results**'. In the early church, the word was not just spoken, but demonstrated. Transformed lives, signs and wonders were its fruit. In Acts19: 20 the scripture says, the **Word of the Lord grew mightily**

and **prevailed**. The Word grew – praise God. It is living. Living things have their own dynamic and grow. The word 'prevailed' has the meaning of manifested power in reigning authority – hallelujah!

God wants the living Word to be released, manifested in and through the lives of each one of us, so revealing His glory. The Word has a mighty active ingredient. If someone takes a pill, it is only the active ingredient that is effective.

How can we let loose the active ingredient inherent in the Word?

We are told to meditate on the word, and this has glorious results (Joshua 1: 8). It was effective under the Old Covenant, much more so now that the Spirit has been released. Col 3: 16 tells us to, 'Let the word of Christ dwell in you richly in all wisdom, teaching and admonishing one another in psalms and hymns and spiritual songs, singing with grace in your hearts to the Lord'.

There are many non-verbal ways we can employ as well. Letting our bodies respond, like raising our hands in worship or dancing like David did, will enhance its meaning for us.

We are told to pray in the spirit, speaking in tongues. This will edify us, build ourselves up (Jude 20), and help us to know the **mysteries** of the living Word (1Cor 14: 2).

Lord, I believe that as I do these things my spirit will be ignited with the very power, the inherent energy of the Word – hallelujah!

Receive

Thank You Lord, that I am a Spirit-filled, born again believer. Thank You that You have made my spirit to receive the living Word of God, so that it can become a living reality, expressed through my life – hallelujah! Yes, I will meditate on your Word, I will possess Your Word, incubate Your Word, and receive it, but not only through my mind...

When I receive a beautiful present from a friend, I may just say, 'thank you', but deep within I am at the same time rejoicing and longing to express love to that person. I may even express that rejoicing with a jump of joy, a wow! My whole being is involved. Such expressions increase the value, the meaning of that present to me, and my relationship with the person who gave it. In the same way, my spirit can respond non-verbally to the Word of God. As I embrace it, delight in it, my body may respond by shaking with joy, which is an expression of my spirit dancing with joy. I may laugh, – why had I not seen that before? – the eyes of my spirit have seen something more of my glorious Lord His love for me, my inheritance – glory to God!

I will pray in tongues. As I do so, focusing on a particular scripture, it will be as if the muscles of that scripture are growing stronger. I can ask God to reveal more about it. While praying in tongues, thoughts will arise about it such as, – 'Yes, this is for you – delight to put it to work – at home'. I will receive a deeper understanding of its **awesome character**, for example, how it cannot fail to work – hallelujah. The Holy Spirit can take hold of that precious Word and reveal it to me as I need it right now – glory to God!

I will dwell in the word richly, delight in it, when by myself and with others. Like Paul, 'I will sing with the spirit, and I will also sing with the understanding (1Cor 14: 15) –– glory to God,

I am being built up.

Live it – language

What joy it will be to talk about the Word, to share the new revelations received and for others to catch its life. My delight in it, my enthusiasm will be so evident. It will be infectious.

Others will sense this dynamic in their spirit and be drawn to know it for themselves and be drawn to You – glory to God. Also, my prayers will be more than just words. They will be rooted from deep within and be effective. They will work – hallelujah!

Live it – lifestyle

I am full of the living Word. Whatever the situation, whatever the problem,

I know that the truth living in me, will release the solution, the wisdom, the love, the healing, the miracle – hallelujah. There is no limit to our God.

Now

Today, I will trust You with all my heart and trust the power of Your life within. Wherever I go, I will be ready to bring life, to be the answer to any problem. I am loaded with the living Word, I am loaded with life. I know there will be many divine encounters.

Many will be blessed by Your life flowing from me.

Triumphantly

What joy is in my spirit. You know the people I will be meeting today. You have planned it all. You know that their lives are going to be transformed through our encounter. You are going to be so glorified today. It will be an exciting day today.

Recommendation on Harriet's teaching

"...... they are pure gold! They put into words all the things I felt the Lord was trying to lead me into, and now I just long to bring others into that wonderful place of freedom you spoke with wisdom ...... This is a fresh experience ...... leaving behind religious bondage and thriving in the truth of His Word.

"Thank you for your ministry. From time to time I turn on Revelation TV hoping you may be speaking words of encouragement ...."

Gina Watson
Frinton-on-Sea.